# Math

3+4=7

CARSON-DELLOSA™
PUBLISHING GROUP

Greensboro, NC 27425 USA

# Table of Contents

Brighter Child®
An imprint of Carson-Dellosa Publishing LLC
P.O. Box 35665
Greensboro, NC 27425  USA

Printed in the USA • All rights reserved.   ISBN  978-1-4838-1651-7

05-198177784

Name_____

# Trace and Write Zero 0

**Directions: Trace** and **write** the number **0**. Then, **draw** an **X** on the tanks with zero fish.

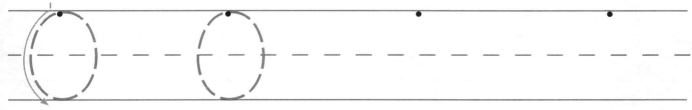

Name _____

# Trace and Write One and Two 1, 2

**Directions: Trace** 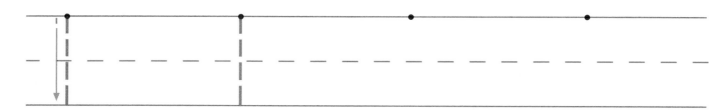 **and write** the numbers **1** and **2**. Then, **count** and **write** the correct number.

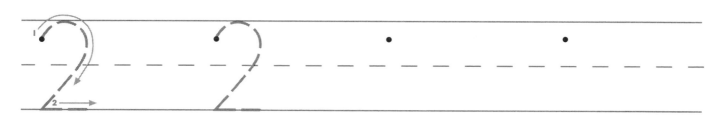

# Trace and Write Three and Four 3, 4

**Directions: Trace** 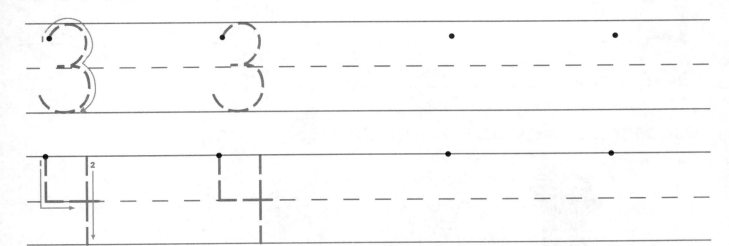 and **write** the numbers **3** and **4**. Then, **count** and **write** the correct number.

_____  _____

# 5 ● ● ● ● ● five

**Directions:** Write  the number **5** on the line 5 times.

# 5 5

**Directions:** 5 dogs are colored. **Color** 🖍 5 dogs.

# Review Numbers 0—5

**Directions: Trace**  the path from 1—5 on each picture.

**Color** the pictures.

# 6 ●●●●●● six

**Directions: Write**  **the number 6 on the line 6 times.**

**Directions: Draw** an **X**  **on each group of six things.**

# Seven and Eight 7, 8

**Directions:** Write  the numbers **7** and **8**.

7 7       8 8

**Directions:** **Count** and **write**  the number of glasses on each line.

_____       _____

- - - - - - -       - - - - - - -

**Directions:** Draw  peas on each plate to show the number.

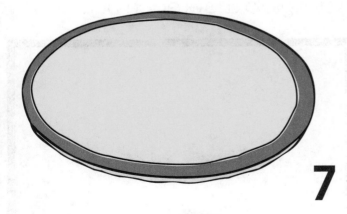

7

8

# Nine and Ten 9, 10

**Directions: Write**  the numbers **9** and **10**.

**Directions: Write**  the number of cupcakes on each line.

**Directions: Draw**  balloons with strings to show each number.

# Review Numbers 6—10

**Directions: Count** the beads in each group. **Write** 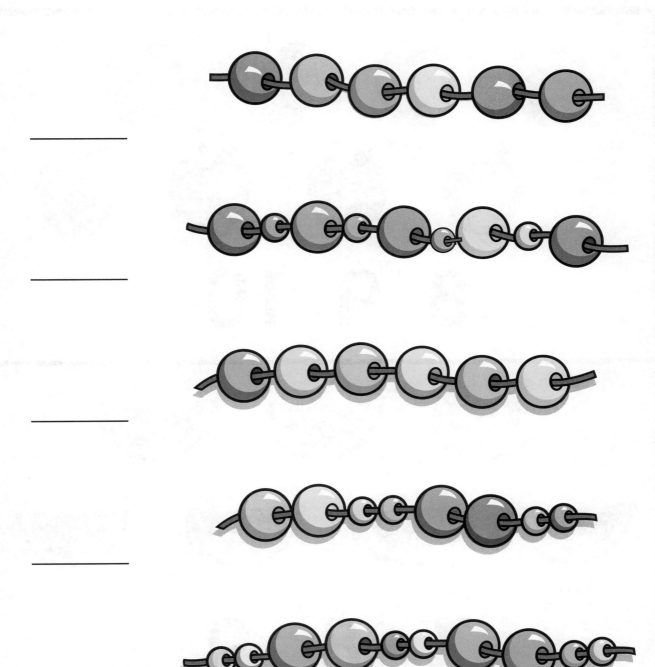 the number.

_____

_____

_____

_____

_____

Name _____

# Review Numbers 6—10

**Directions: Circle**  the correct number in each box.

Name _____

# Review Numbers 0—10

**Directions: Draw** an **X** 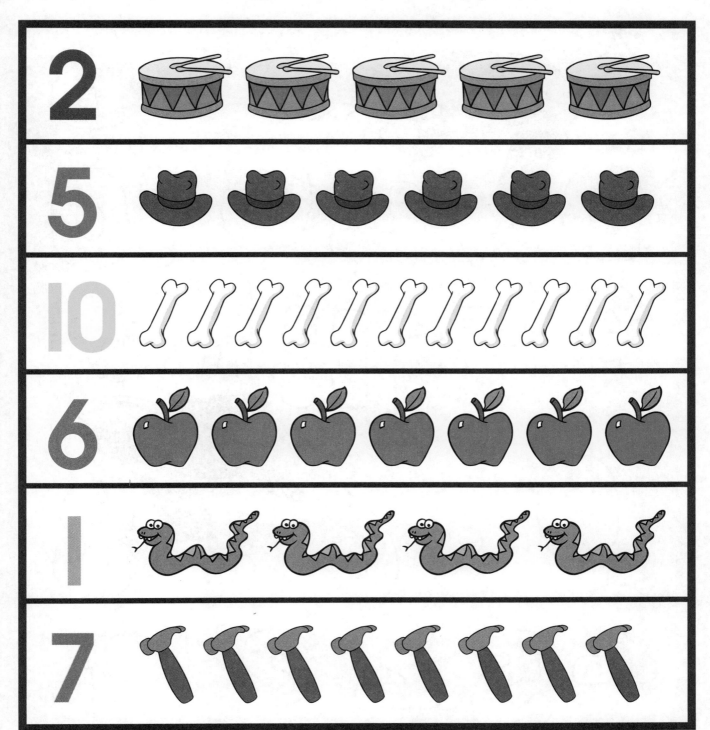 on the extra things in each row.

# Review Numbers 0—10

**Directions: Color**  each number. **Draw** an **X** on each letter.

Name _____

# Trace and Write Eleven and Twelve 11, 12

**Directions: Trace** 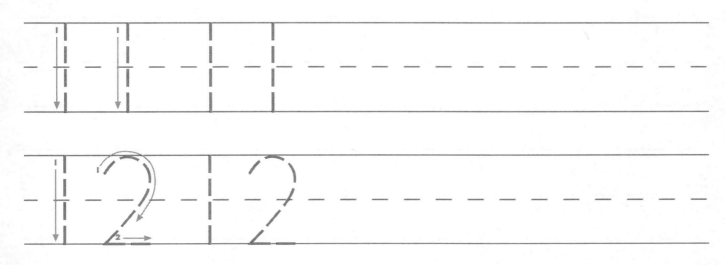 **and write** the numbers 11 and 12. Then, **count** and **write** the numbers.

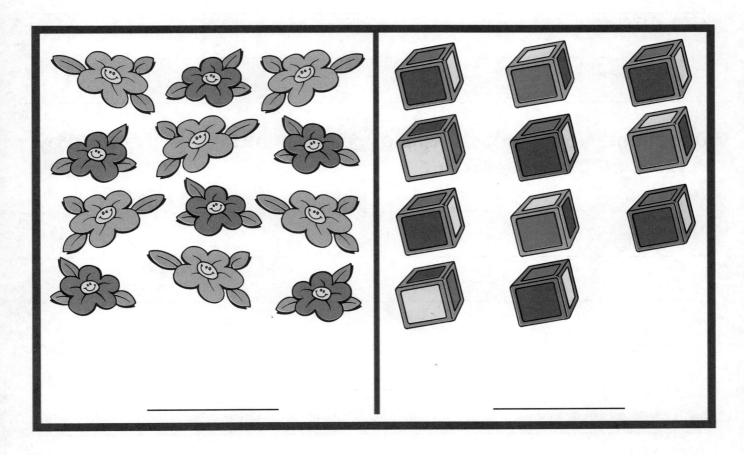

_____     _____

# Trace and Write Thirteen 13

**Directions: Trace** 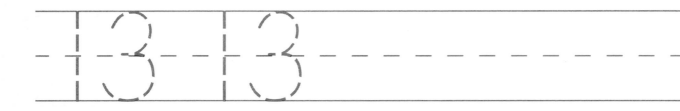 **and write** the number **13** and the number word.

13  13

thirteen

thirteen

**Directions:** Now practice **writing** the **number** and the **word** by yourself on the lines below.

# Trace and Write Fourteen 14

**Directions: Trace** 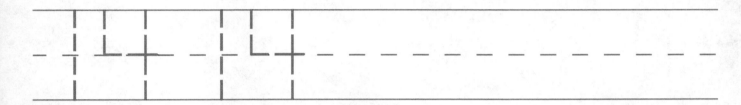 and **write** the number 14 and the number word.

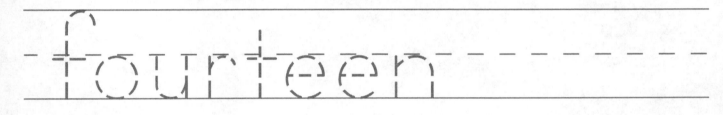

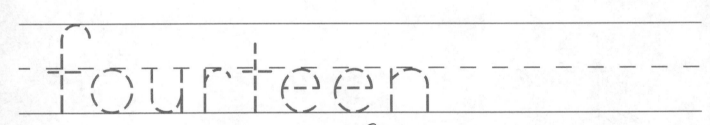

**Directions:** Now practice **writing** the **number** and the **word** by yourself on the lines below.

# Trace and Write Fifteen 15

**Directions: Trace** and **write** the number **15** and the number word.

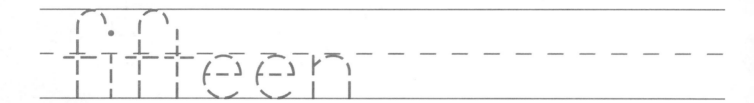

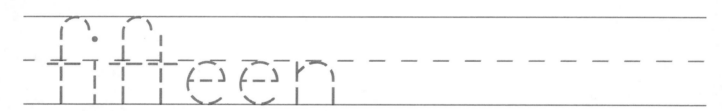

**Directions:** Now practice **writing** the **number** and the **word** by yourself on the lines below.

# Trace and Write Sixteen 16

**Directions: Trace** 🖉 **and write** 🖉 the number **16** and the number word.

16  16

sixteen

sixteen

**Directions:** Now practice **writing** 🖉 the **number** and the **word** by yourself on the lines below.

# Trace and Write Seventeen 17

**Directions: Trace**  and **write** the number **17** and the number word.

17 17 17

seventeen

seventeen

**Directions:** Now practice **writing** 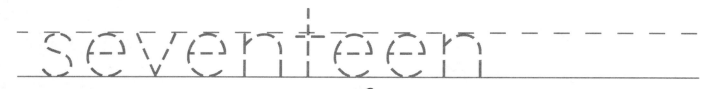 the **number** and the **word** by yourself on the lines below.

# Trace and Write Eighteen 18

**Directions: Trace** 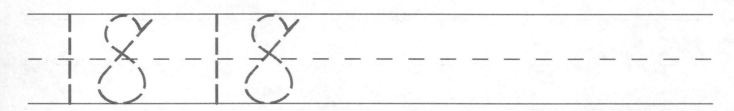 **and write** the number **18** and the number word.

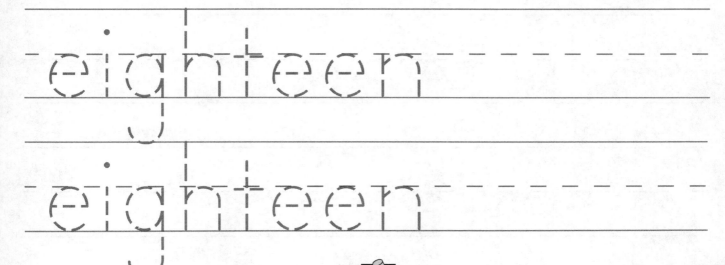

**Directions:** Now practice **writing** the **number** and the **word** by yourself on the lines below.

# Trace and Write Nineteen 19

**Directions: Trace** and **write** the number 19 and the number word.

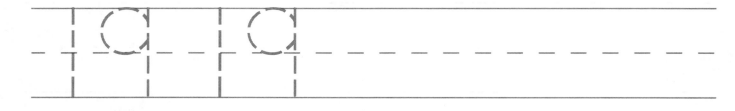

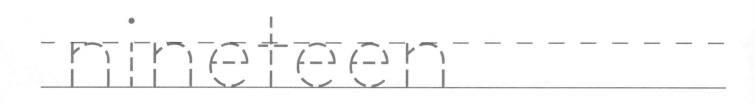

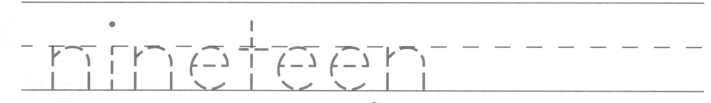

**Directions:** Now practice **writing** the **number** and the **word** by yourself on the lines below.

# Trace and Write Twenty 20

**Directions:** Trace 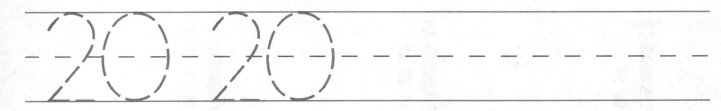 and **write** the number **20** and the number word.

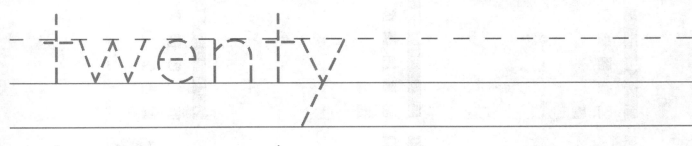

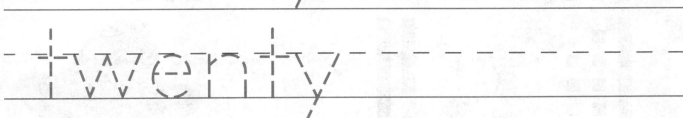

**Directions:** Now practice **writing** the **number** and the **word** by yourself on the lines below.

# Review Numbers 13—20

**Directions: Count** the cubes. **Trace** the number that tells how many.

# Review Numbers 0—20

**Directions: Count** the first row of beads. **Circle** 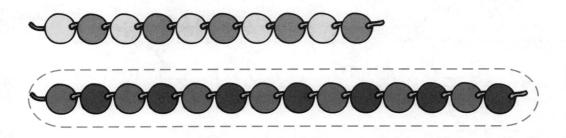 the next row of beads to show that it has more than 10 beads. **Circle** the rows of beads with more than 10.

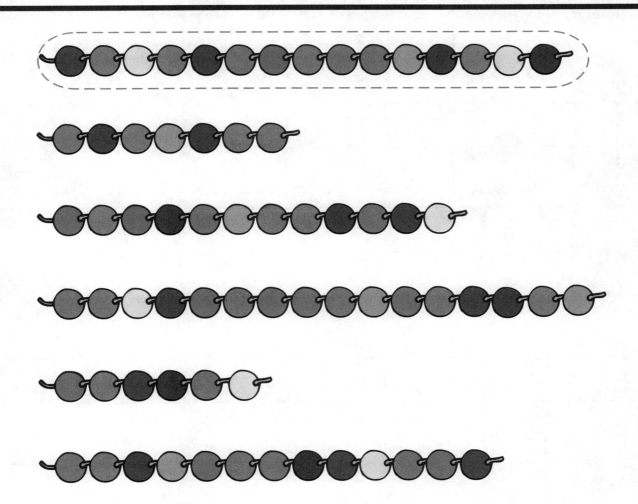

Name_____

# Review Numbers 0—20

**Directions:** Practice writing **0—20**. Trace  the numbers and the words.

0    1    2    3    4

5    6    7    8    9

10    11    12    13

14    15    16    17

18    19    20

zero one two

three four

*Math: Kindergarten*

Name_____

# Review Numbers 0—20

**Directions: Trace**  the number words.

five    six    seven

eight    nine    ten

eleven    twelve

thirteen    fourteen

fifteen    sixteen

seventeen    eighteen

nineteen    twenty

# Missing Numbers

**Directions: Write**  the missing number in each box on the blackboard. The first one has been done for you.

2, **3** , 4

8, 9, ___

___ , 6, 7

0, ___ , 2

4, 5, ___

6, 7, ___

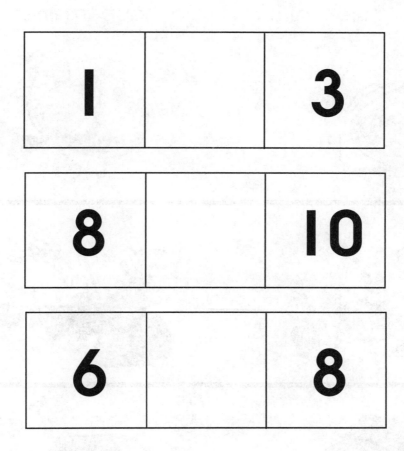

# Missing Numbers

**Directions: Write**  the missing number in each box.

| 1 | | 3 |

| 8 | | 10 |

| 6 | | 8 |

**Directions: Circle** the number that is **smaller** in each pair.

| 10    4 | | 2    7 | | 5    1 |

# Order Events

**Directions:** Which comes **first**, the chick hatching or the egg cracking?

**Circle**  the picture that shows what happens **first**.

# First

**Directions:** Look at the pictures. Which happened **first** in each row?

**Circle**  the picture that shows what happened **first**.

# Next

**Directions: Circle**  the picture that shows what comes next.

# Sequencing

**Directions:** Write  **1**, **2**, and **3** in the boxes to show what happens **first**, **second**, and **third**.

# Sequencing

**Directions: Write**  **1, 2, 3,** and **4** in the boxes to show the correct order to tell the story.

# Ordinal Numbers

**Directions: Color**  the **first** leaf **red**. **Circle** the **third** leaf.

**Directions: Color** the **fourth** balloon **purple**. **Draw** a line under the **second** balloon.

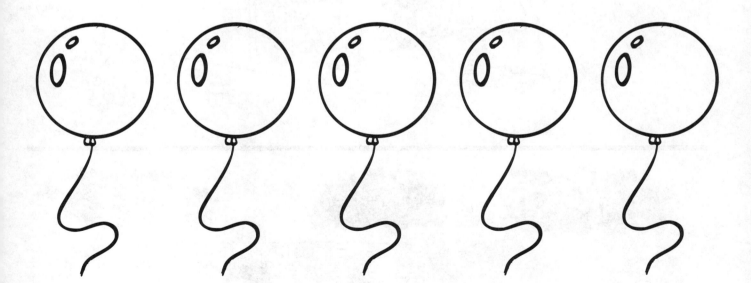

# Last

**Directions:** Circle  the **last** thing in each row.

Name _____

# More

**Directions: Color**  the group in each box that has **more**.

# Fewer

**Directions: Count** the cars on the top road.

On the bottom road, **draw**  **fewer** cars than on the top road.

# Shape Patterns

**Directions: Draw** 🖍 **and color** 🖍 the shape that comes next in each pattern.

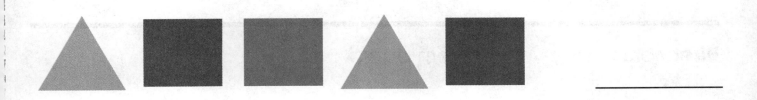

# Perfect Patterns

**Directions:** Use a **crayon**  or a **pencil** to make a copy of this pattern.

**Directions:** Copy the pattern above backwards.

**Directions:** Now design a pattern of your own!

**Directions:** Copy your pattern backwards.

# Number Patterns

**Directions: Copy**  the number pattern in each row.

1 5 1 5 1 5

2 9 2 9 2 9

8 8 4 8 8 4

# Brothers and Sisters

**Directions:** Find the brothers and sisters in the Green Swamp. They have the same shapes and the same patterns on their bodies.

**Draw**  a line from each brother on the top leaf to his sister on the bottom leaf.

# Above and Below

**Directions: Circle**  the picture that is **above** the others.

**Draw** an **X** on the picture that is **below** the others.

# Above and Below

**Directions: Color**  the pictures **above** the clouds first. Then, **color** the pictures **below** the clouds.

# Between

**Directions: Trace**  and **color** the cat that is **between** the other cats.

**Directions: Color** the mouse that is **between** the other mice.

**45**  *Math: Kindergarten*

# Between

**Directions: Color** 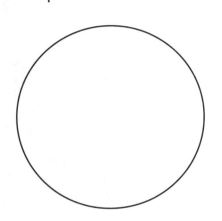 each shape that is **between** the other shapes.

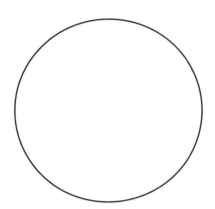
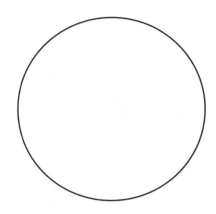

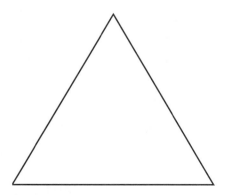
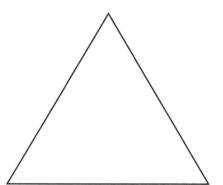
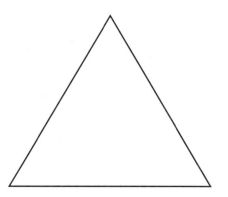

# Left and Right

**Directions: Color**  the pictures on the **left blue. Color** the pictures on the **right red.**

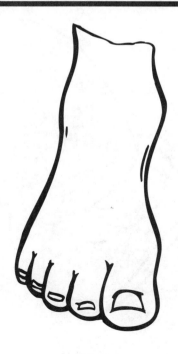
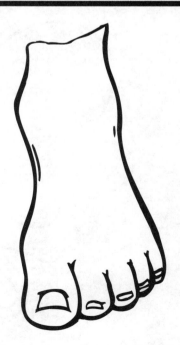

# Left and Right

**Directions: Color** 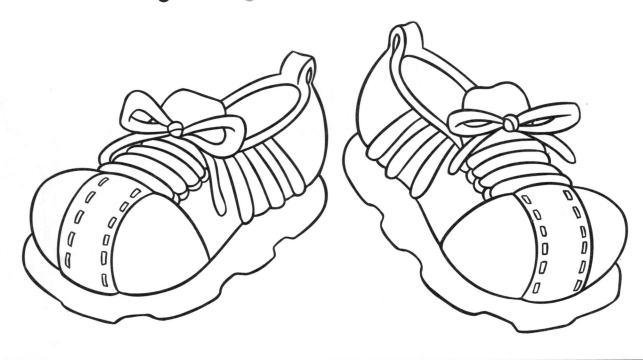 the pictures on the **left green**. **Color** the pictures on the **right orange**.

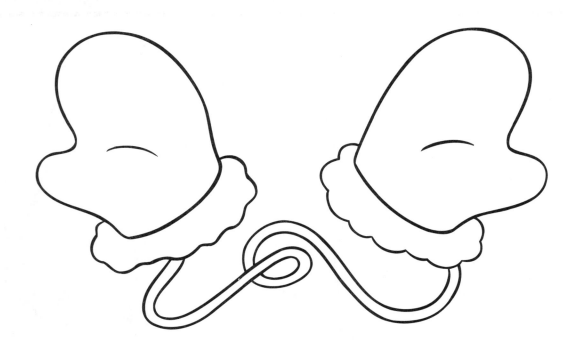

# Graphing

**Directions: Count** the boxes.

How many of each vehicle? **Write**  the numbers.

  2

 _____

 _____

 _____

*Math: Kindergarten*

# Graphing

**Directions: Count** the pets in the window. Then, **color**  one box for each animal on the graph below.

# Lots of Boxes

**Directions: Connect**  the dots with a **red** crayon and make the biggest square you can. **Connect** the dots with a **blue** crayon and make the smallest square you can. Now, use different-colored crayons to make more squares.

# Erase a Shape

Milo and Veronica are playing a shape game. They want you to play, too! Milo draws a figure made of two shapes. Veronica erases one of the shapes.

**Directions:** Use a crayon to **draw** the shape that is left. The first one has been done for you.

| Milo draws: | Veronica erases: | The shape left: |
|---|---|---|

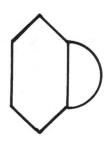

# Add a Shape

Suji and Cosmos are playing a shape game. Suji draws a shape. Cosmos adds another shape to make a figure with two shapes. What shape does Cosmos add each time?

**Directions: Draw** 🖊 the shape Cosmos adds. The first one has been done for you.

| Suji draws: | Cosmos adds: | The new shape: |
|:---:|:---:|:---:|
|  |  | 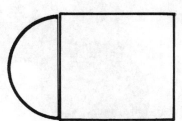 |
|  | |  |
|  | | 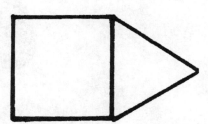 |

*Math: Kindergarten*

# The Whole Shape

Jag has drawn pictures of different shapes, but each shape is only half done!

**Directions: Draw**  the missing half to complete each shape.

# The Whole Shape

**Directions: Draw**  the missing half to complete each shape.

**55**  *Math: Kindergarten*

# Play Blocks

The monster babies are playing with blocks. Each block has **two** equal parts.

**Directions: Color** 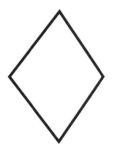 each part a different color.

 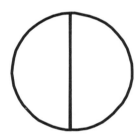

 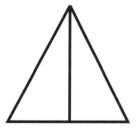

**Directions:** Divide this block into **two** equal parts. **Color** each part a different color.

**56**

*Math: Kindergarten*

# Best Friends

Maggie and Babs are best friends. They share many things. Divide each kind of food below so that Maggie and Babs each get the same amount.

**Directions: Circle**  Maggie's food with a **blue** crayon.
**Circle** Babs's food with a **red** crayon.

Name _____

# Split in Two

How many equal parts?

2

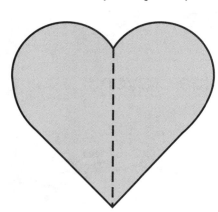
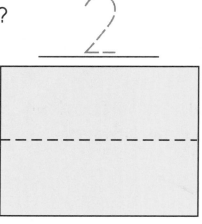
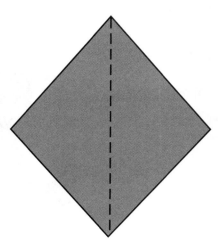

**Directions: Color**  **shapes with 2 equal parts.**

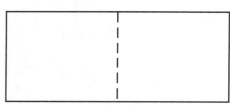
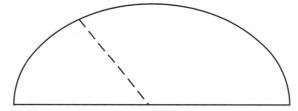

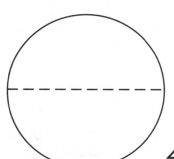
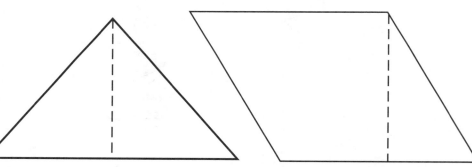

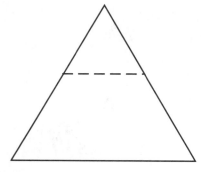
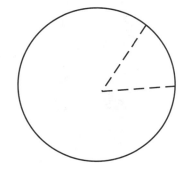
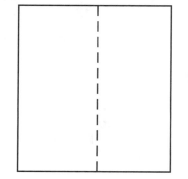

# Clock Numbers

**Directions: Trace**  the numbers I—12 in order on the clock.

Hickory Dickory Dock,
The mouse ran up the clock.
The clock struck one and down he ran.
Hickory Dickory Dock.

*Math: Kindergarten*

# What Time Is It?

Mrs. Murky is teaching the monsters how to tell time. She shows them this clock, which says it's **2** o'clock.

**Directions:** Look at the hands on the clock. They point to numbers. One hand is longer. It's called the **big hand**. The other hand is shorter. It's called the **small hand**. We know it is 2 o'clock because the big hand is pointing to **12** and the small hand is pointing to the **2**.

# Maggie and Didi

**Directions: Write**  the time Maggie and Didi do each thing on the line below each picture.

_____ o'clock

_____ o'clock

_____ o'clock

_____ o'clock

# Reading a Clock

Help the monsters tell time by completing the clocks below.

**Directions: Draw**  a **small hand** on each clock to show what time it is.

1 o'clock

3 o'clock

6 o'clock

# More Clocks

**Directions:** Draw a **small hand** on each clock to show what time it is.

8 o'clock

10 o'clock

12 o'clock

# Pennies

A penny is worth 1¢. It is brown.

**Directions: Circle**  the correct amount of money in each row below. The first one is done for you.

      1¢ （2¢） 3¢

     1¢ 2¢ 3¢

       5¢ 6¢ 7¢

         7¢ 8¢ 9¢

# Nickels

A nickel is worth **5¢**. It is silver.

**Directions: Circle**  the correct amount of money in each row below.

5¢ = 5¢

---

         4¢  5¢  6¢

---

          1¢  2¢  3¢

---

         1¢  2¢  3¢

Name_____

# Dimes

A dime is worth **10¢**. It is silver.

**Directions: Circle** 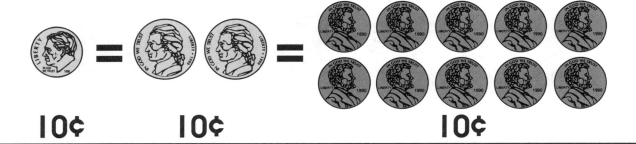 the correct amount of money in each row below.

10¢          10¢                    10¢

---

          1¢   5¢   10¢

---

           5¢   7¢   10¢

---

          8¢   9¢   10¢

Name _____

# Penny, Nickel, Dime

**Directions: Color**  each penny brown. **Draw** a line under each nickel. Draw a **circle** around each dime.

penny          nickel          dime

# Review Money

**Directions:** Draw  a line to match the price of the thing to the correct amount of money.

# Rimsley's Piggy Bank

Rimsley has saved a lot of money. This is the kind of money he has saved:

**penny**          **nickel**          **dime**

**Directions:**   Color all the **pennies** in the bank **brown**.
Color all the **nickels** in the bank **red**.
Color all the **dimes** in the bank **blue**.

# Lemonade Stand

Cosmos is selling lemonade. The other monsters want to buy some. The lemonade costs **10¢**, or **10 pennies**. Do the monsters have enough money to buy lemonade? Read the clues below to find out.

**Directions: Write**  your answers on the lines. A nickel is the same as **5** pennies.

Hugh has **4** pennies and **1** nickel.
How much more money does he need? _____

Rimsley has **6** pennies.
How much more money does he need? _____

Ursula has **2** pennies and **1** nickel.
How much more money does she need? _____

# Answer Key

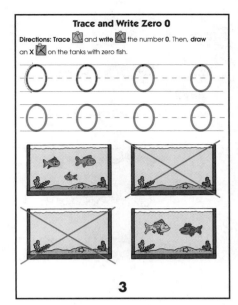

**Trace and Write Zero 0**

**Directions:** Trace and write the number 0. Then, **draw** an **X** on the tanks with zero fish.

3

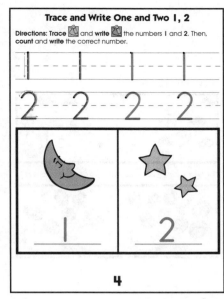

**Trace and Write One and Two 1, 2**

**Directions:** Trace and write the numbers 1 and 2. Then, **count** and **write** the correct number.

4

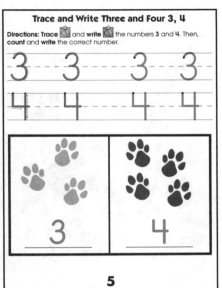

**Trace and Write Three and Four 3, 4**

**Directions:** Trace and **write** the numbers 3 and 4. Then, **count** and **write** the correct number.

5

**5 ●●●●● five**

**Directions:** Write the number 5 on the line 5 times.

**Directions:** 5 dogs are colored. **Color** 5 dogs.

6

**Review Numbers 0—5**

**Directions:** Trace the path from 1–5 on each picture. **Color** the pictures.

7

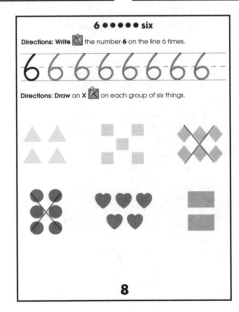

**6 ●●●●● six**

**Directions:** Write the number 6 on the line 6 times.

**Directions:** Draw an **X** on each group of six things.

8

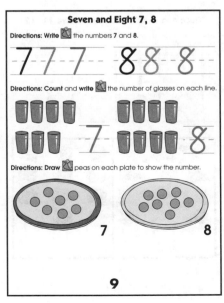

**Seven and Eight 7, 8**

**Directions:** Write the numbers 7 and 8.

**Directions: Count** and **write** the number of glasses on each line.

**Directions:** Draw peas on each plate to show the number.

9

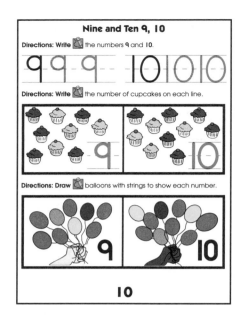

### Nine and Ten 9, 10

**Directions:** Write the numbers 9 and 10.

9 9 9    10 10 10

**Directions:** Write the number of cupcakes on each line.

9    10

**Directions:** Draw balloons with strings to show each number.

9    10

10

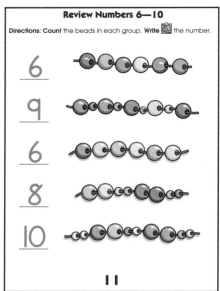

### Review Numbers 6—10

**Directions:** Count the beads in each group. Write the number.

6
9
6
8
10

11

### Review Numbers 6—10

**Directions:** Circle the correct number in each box.

⑧ 9 10

⑦ 8 9

12

### Review Numbers 0—10

**Directions:** Draw an X on the extra things in each row.

2
5
10
6
1
7

13

### Review Numbers 0—10

**Directions:** Color each number. Draw an X on each letter.

14

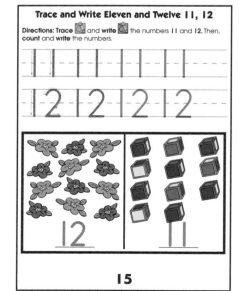

### Trace and Write Eleven and Twelve 11, 12

**Directions:** Trace and write the numbers 11 and 12. Then, **count** and **write** the numbers.

11 11 11 11 11

12 12 12 12

12    11

15

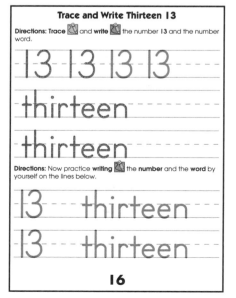

### Trace and Write Thirteen 13

**Directions:** Trace and write the number 13 and the number word.

13 13 13 13

thirteen

thirteen

**Directions:** Now practice **writing** the **number** and the **word** by yourself on the lines below.

13 — thirteen

13 — thirteen

16

**Trace and Write Fourteen 14**

Directions: Trace 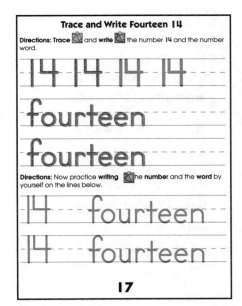 and write the number 14 and the number word.

14 14 14 14

fourteen

fourteen

Directions: Now practice **writing** the **number** and the **word** by yourself on the lines below.

14    fourteen

14    fourteen

**17**

---

**Trace and Write Fifteen 15**

Directions: Trace and write the number 15 and the number word.

15 15 15 15

fifteen

fifteen

Directions: Now practice **writing** the **number** and the **word** by yourself on the lines below.

15    fifteen

15    fifteen

**18**

---

**Trace and Write Sixteen 16**

Directions: Trace 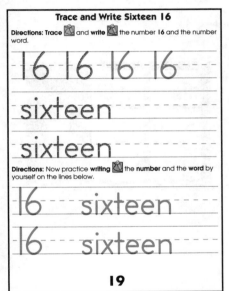 and write the number 16 and the number word.

16 16 16 16

sixteen

sixteen

Directions: Now practice **writing** the **number** and the **word** by yourself on the lines below.

16    sixteen

16    sixteen

**19**

---

**Trace and Write Seventeen 17**

Directions: Trace and write the number 17 and the number word.

17 17 17 17

seventeen

seventeen

Directions: Now practice **writing** the **number** and the **word** by yourself on the lines below.

17    seventeen

17    seventeen

**20**

---

**Trace and Write Eighteen 18**

Directions: Trace and write the number 18 and the number word.

18 18 18 18

eighteen

eighteen

Directions: Now practice **writing** the **number** and the **word** by yourself on the lines below.

18    eighteen

18    eighteen

**21**

---

**Trace and Write Nineteen 19**

Directions: Trace and write the number 19 and the number word.

19 19 19 19

nineteen

nineteen

Directions: Now practice **writing** the **number** and the **word** by yourself on the lines below.

19    nineteen

19    nineteen

**22**

---

**Trace and Write Twenty 20**

Directions: Trace and write the number 20 and the number word.

20 20 20 20

twenty

twenty

Directions: Now practice **writing** the **number** and the **word** by yourself on the lines below.

20    twenty

20    twenty

**23**

---

*Math: Kindergarten*

### Review Numbers 13—20

**Directions: Count** the cubes. **Trace** 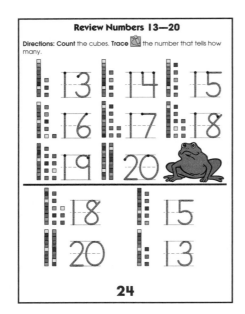 the number that tells how many.

### Review Numbers 0—20

**Directions: Count** the first row of beads. **Circle** the next row of beads to show that it has more than 10 beads. **Circle** the rows of beads with more than 10.

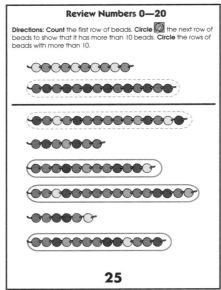

**24**

**25**

### Review Numbers 0—20

**Directions: Practice** writing **0–20. Trace** the numbers and the words.

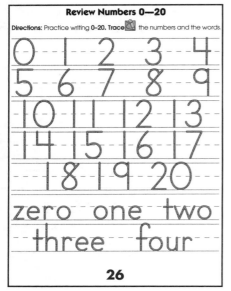

**26**

### Review Numbers 0—20

**Directions: Trace** the number words.

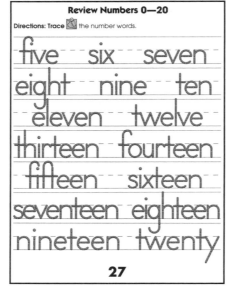

**27**

### Missing Numbers

**Directions: Write** the missing number in each box on the blackboard. The first one has been done for you.

**28**

### Missing Numbers

**Directions: Write** the missing number in each box.

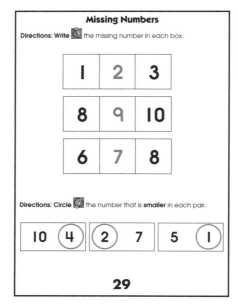

**Directions: Circle** the number that is **smaller** in each pair.

**29**

### Order Events

**Directions:** Which comes **first**, the chick hatching or the egg cracking?

**Circle** the picture that shows what happens **first**.

**30**

## First

**Directions:** Look at the pictures. Which happened **first** in each row? **Circle**  the picture that shows what happened **first.**

## Next

**Directions: Circle** the picture that shows what comes next.

## Sequencing

**Directions: Write** 1, 2, and 3 in the boxes to show what happens **first, second,** and **third.**

## Sequencing

**Directions: Write** 1, 2, 3, and 4 in the boxes to show the correct order to tell the story.

## Ordinal Numbers

**Directions: Color** the **first** leaf red. **Circle** the **third** leaf.

**Directions: Color** the **fourth** balloon purple. **Draw** a line under the **second** balloon.

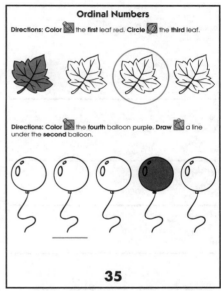

## Last

**Directions: Circle** the **last** thing in each row.

## More

**Directions: Color** the group in each box that has **more.**

## Fewer

**Directions: Count** the cars on the top road.

On the bottom road, **draw**  **fewer** cars than on the top road.

**38**

## Shape Patterns

**Directions: Draw** 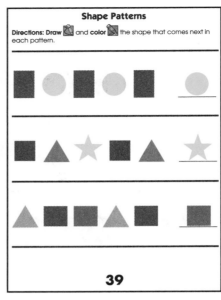 and **color** the shape that comes next in each pattern.

**39**

## Perfect Patterns

**Directions:** Use a **crayon** or a **pencil** to make a copy of this pattern.

**Directions:** Copy the pattern above backwards.

**Directions:** Now design a pattern of your own!

Answers will vary.

**Directions:** Copy your pattern backwards.

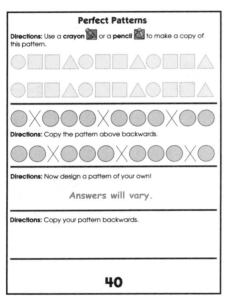

**40**

## Number Patterns

**Directions: Copy** the number pattern in each row.

| 1 | 5 | 1 | 5 | 1 | 5 |
| 1 | 5 | 1 | 5 | 1 | 5 |
| 2 | 9 | 2 | 9 | 2 | 9 |
| 2 | 9 | 2 | 9 | 2 | 9 |
| 8 | 8 | 4 | 8 | 8 | 4 |
| 8 | 8 | 4 | 8 | 8 | 4 |

**41**

## Brothers and Sisters

**Directions:** Find the brothers and sisters in the Green Swamp. They have the same shapes and the same patterns on their bodies.

**Draw** a line from each brother on the top leaf to his sister on the bottom leaf.

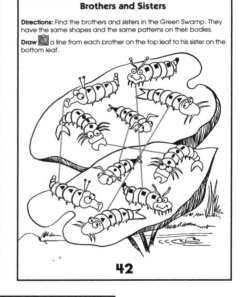

**42**

## Above and Below

**Directions: Circle** the picture that is **above** the others.

**Draw an X** on the picture that is **below** the others.

**43**

## Above and Below

**Directions: Color** the pictures **above** the clouds first. Then, **color** the pictures **below** the clouds.

First

First

Second

Second

**44**

## Between

**Directions: Trace**  and **color** the cat that is **between** the other cats.

**Directions: Color** the mouse that is **between** the other mice.

**45**

## Between

**Directions: Color** each shape that is **between** the other shapes.

**46**

## Left and Right

**Directions: Color** the pictures on the **left** blue. **Color** the pictures on the **right** red.

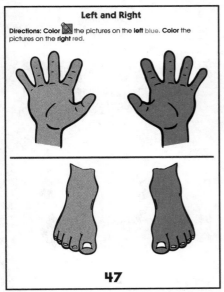

**47**

## Left and Right

**Directions: Color** the pictures on the **left** green. **Color** the pictures on the **right** orange.

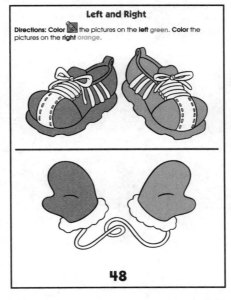

**48**

## Graphing

**Directions: Count** the boxes.

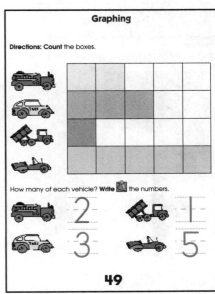

How many of each vehicle? **Write** the numbers.

2   1

3   5

**49**

## Graphing

**Directions: Count** the pets in the window. Then, **color** one box for each animal on the graph below.

**50**

## Lots of Boxes

**Directions: Connect** the dots with a red crayon and make the biggest square you can. **Connect** the dots with a blue crayon and make the smallest square you can. Now, use different-colored crayons to make more squares.

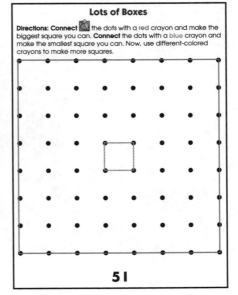

**51**

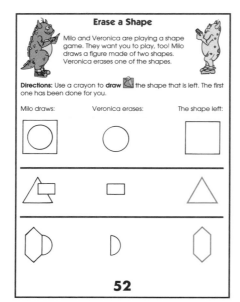

### Erase a Shape

Milo and Veronica are playing a shape game. They want you to play, too! Milo draws a figure made of two shapes. Veronica erases one of the shapes.

**Directions:** Use a crayon to **draw** the shape that is left. The first one has been done for you.

Milo draws:    Veronica erases:    The shape left:

**52**

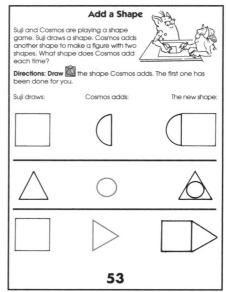

### Add a Shape

Suji and Cosmos are playing a shape game. Suji draws a shape. Cosmos adds another shape to make a figure with two shapes. What shape does Cosmos add each time?

**Directions:** Draw the shape Cosmos adds. The first one has been done for you.

Suji draws:    Cosmos adds:    The new shape:

**53**

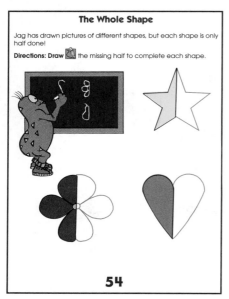

### The Whole Shape

Jag has drawn pictures of different shapes, but each shape is only half done!

**Directions:** Draw the missing half to complete each shape.

**54**

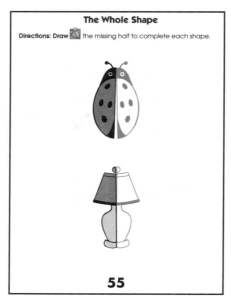

### The Whole Shape

**Directions:** Draw the missing half to complete each shape.

**55**

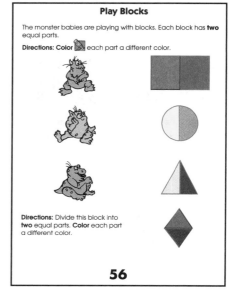

### Play Blocks

The monster babies are playing with blocks. Each block has **two** equal parts.

**Directions:** Color each part a different color.

**Directions:** Divide this block into **two** equal parts. **Color** each part a different color.

**56**

### Best Friends

Maggie and Babs are best friends. They share many things. Divide each kind of food below so that Maggie and Babs each get the same amount.

**Directions:** Circle Maggie's food with a blue crayon. **Circle** Babs' food with a red crayon.

**57**

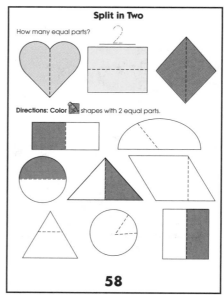

### Split in Two

How many equal parts?

**Directions:** Color shapes with 2 equal parts.

**58**

## Clock Numbers

**Directions:** Trace  the numbers 1–12 in order on the clock.

Hickory Dickory Dock,
The mouse ran up the clock.
The clock struck one and down he ran.
Hickory Dickory Dock.

**59**

## What Time Is It?

Mrs. Murky is teaching the monsters how to tell time. She shows them this clock, which says it's **2 o'clock**.

**Directions:** Look at the hands on the clock. They point to numbers. One hand is longer. It's called the **big hand**. The other hand is shorter. It's called the **small hand**. We know it is 2 o'clock because the big hand is pointing to **12** and the small hand is pointing to the **2**.

**60**

## Maggie and Didi

**Directions:** Write  the time Maggie and Didi do each thing on the line below each picture.

_____ o'clock     **2** _____ o'clock

**5** _____ o'clock     **8** _____ o'clock

**61**

## Reading a Clock

Help the monsters tell time by completing the clocks below.

**Directions:** Draw 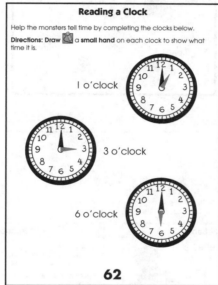 a **small hand** on each clock to show what time it is.

1 o'clock

3 o'clock

6 o'clock

**62**

## More Clocks

**Directions:** Draw 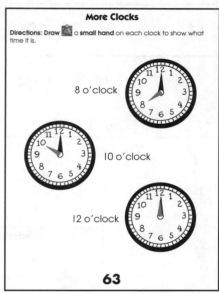 a **small hand** on each clock to show what time it is.

8 o'clock

10 o'clock

12 o'clock

**63**

## Pennies

A penny is worth **1¢**. It is brown.

**Directions:** Circle 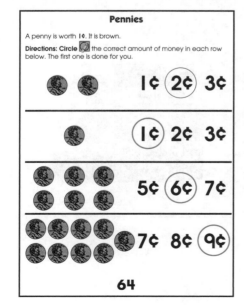 the correct amount of money in each row below. The first one is done for you.

1¢　(2¢)　3¢

(1¢)　2¢　3¢

5¢　(6¢)　7¢

7¢　8¢　(9¢)

**64**

## Nickels

A nickel is worth **5¢**. It is silver.

**Directions:** Circle 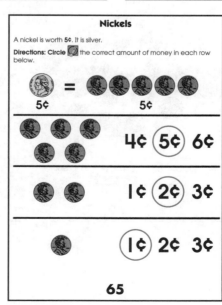 the correct amount of money in each row below.

5¢　=　5¢

4¢　(5¢)　6¢

1¢　(2¢)　3¢

(1¢)　2¢　3¢

**65**

## Dimes

A dime is worth **10¢**. It is silver.

**Directions: Circle** 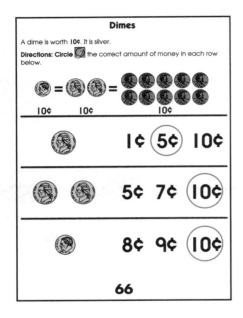 the correct amount of money in each row below.

66

## Penny, Nickel, Dime

**Directions: Color** each penny brown. **Draw** a line under each nickel. Draw a **circle** around each dime.

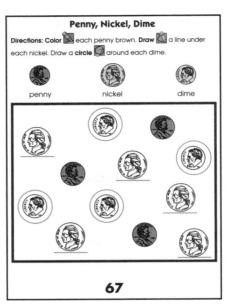

penny          nickel          dime

67

## Review Money

**Directions: Draw** a line to match the price of the thing to the correct amount of money.

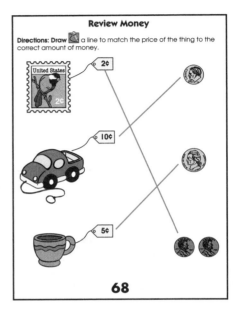

United States 2¢

10¢

5¢

68

## Rimsley's Piggy Bank

Rimsley has saved a lot of money. This is the kind of money he has saved:

penny          nickel          dime

**Directions: Color** all the **pennies** in the bank **brown**.
**Color** all the **nickels** in the bank **red**.
**Color** all the **dimes** in the bank **blue**.

69

## Lemonade Stand

Cosmos is selling lemonade. The other monsters want to buy some. The lemonade costs **10¢**, or **10 pennies**. Do the monsters have enough money to buy lemonade? Read the clues below to find out.

**Directions: Write** your answers on the lines. A nickel is the same as **5** pennies.

Hugh has **4** pennies and **1** nickel.
How much more money does he need?          **1 ¢**

Rimsley has **6** pennies.
How much more money does he need?          **4 ¢**

Ursula has **2** pennies and **1** nickel.
How much more money does she need?          **3 ¢**

70